I Crowned
My Damn Self

I Crowned
My Damn Self

Tamara T. Allen

authorHOUSE®

AuthorHouse™
1663 Liberty Drive
Bloomington, IN 47403
www.authorhouse.com
Phone: 1-800-839-8640

Published by AuthorHouse   04/13/2012

ISBN: 978-1-4685-5260-7 (sc)
ISBN: 978-1-4685-5258-4 (hc)
ISBN: 978-1-4685-5259-1 (e)

I would like to give all respect to my parents Gail & Richard Allen, and my younger sister, Catherine Allen-Franklin. They are my backbone and support system. I love and appreciate your support!

I would like to dedicate my first publication to my beloved friends who are no longer with me: Lionel K. Smith, Michael Calhoun, Tellus J. Colvin, and Otis Lee Bolden. Your murders were the reason my pen bleeds with expressions and lessons I learned from your too early departures.

Contents

RADICAL THOUGHTS

The Grid

Probable cause
To attempt to change the laws
Unjust sentencing
Murder the most heinous crime
Judges take bribes
134 years for armed robbery
23 years for 2nd degree murder
Souls stuck in purgatory
What's more gory?
Death toll in Indonesia
Car's brother's murders'
Unsolved mysteries
Closed cases
Presidential Debating
Gay's liberating
Tourist trips to space
Just smacked you in the face
A robot dancing on mars
Sending back data
People just chatter, no stand up action
Why?
Like T.I. said watch what you say
Might just get locked away
Political prisoner Assasta Shakur

Do your research, racism overt
Don't be fooled by the Presidential selection
Like condoms, use protection
Vote in all areas, not just the presidency
Then we can claim head of household
Like on tax forms
To a small extent we win
Until Electoral College factors in
Back to the begin
Un-just.

Damn It!

You Damn Right I'm a Radical!
Philosophical, & Analytical
With precise observation
We might save civilization
THEN . . . maybe not
Pollution, Evolution of man
Wears, and Tears
Extinct Polar Bears
Giraffe's, and Hippo's
Gain Weight, Get LYPO
Suction
Babies bypass like periods
Lucky Idiots, Hit the Lottery
then go broke
"Nigga's' Complain, then don't Vote
Many voted, but still Died
2 shots, and you lived
2 shots, he said good-bye
What's a cookie with no Chocolate chips?
Here's a Tip, Heads or Tails
Tails follow Heads
Flip the Quarter don't Worry!!!

Dust

Rebel with a Cause
Society never my downfall
I'll never crawl
Beg for mercy
Take my head
Truth I'll never denounce
I pronounced
All accusations correctly
CIA controls illegal drug distribution
Implemented chips for population control
Clinton Correction Facility
Targets non-violent drug abusers
New Age Slavery

Where is the New Age Bravery!
Bobby Seals, Malcolm X, and Marcus Garvey
Todays
Names I won't display
Who enormously give back to charity
Finance education, stability, and future growth in Africa
What about AMERICA?

Our Ancestors still shout for their toil, un-paid wages
Exploited dummy stages
Set up of the Black Panther Party
Syphilis tested on Blacks
How do we get our real last names back?
NEVER
Bloodline lost, how do you re-pay that loss?

Mission Accomplished

TRUTH HURTS
EXPECIALLY WHEN WHITE IS ALWAYS RIGHT
ALEXANDER THE GREAT
AMERICA THE GREAT
GET IT? JOKES OVER!

NEOPOLAN, JOESPH STALIN & HITLER
MESSANGERS OF EARTH & WATER
SET OUT TO CONQUER MANKIND
SO, WHY ARE WE SO BLIND?
NIEVE TO OUR GOVERNMENTS CONSPIRACY TO ENSLAVE
US ALL
AS IF IT HASN'T HAPPENED IN PAST YEARS

WHO NEEDS A HISTORY LESSON
DEMOCRACY IS A LIE
A LITTLE FREEDOM KEEPS US SHY FROM TRUTH
DICTATORSHIP REPRESENTS THE REMAINS OF SURVIVORS
WHO WERE STARVEN, BEATEN, RAVISHED & RAPED!

THE PRESIDENT DOESN'T WATCH HIS SHEEP
HE IS A MEIR TOOL, SIMULAR TO A FOOL
PLEASANTLY PUT A **"SPOKESPERSON"**

"OBAMA O8"
I'M GLAD TO SEE
ONLY DUE TO MISSION ACCOMPLISHED
JUST BECAUSE HE RESEMBLES ME
I MUST STILL SPREAD TRUTH
HE REPRESENTS THE **"LESSER OF TWO EVILS"**
SO, WE MUST STAY DOWN
MY PEOPLE GET OUT AND VOTE
NOT FOR HILARY CLINTON,
BUT, FOR THE MISSION ACCOMPLISHED
THE DAY EVERY SLAVE DIED TO SEE, EQUALITY
THEN, AFTER THE PRESIDENTIAL CAMPAIGN
YOUR FUTURE IS STILL THEIR'S TO CLAIM!

*** I put this excerpt here from a book called *A Racial Programme for the Twentieth Century* by Israel Cohen in 1913. This is an example of how race have been used to manipulate the masses throughout the years. ***

"We must realize that our party's most powerful weapon is racial-tension. By propounding into the consciousness of the dark races, that for centuries they have been oppressed by the Whites, we can move them to the program of the communist party. In America; we will aim for subtle victory. While inflaming the Negro minority against the Whites; we will instill the whites a guilt—complex for their exploitation of the Negroes. We will aid the Negroes to rise to prominence in every walk of life, in the professions, and in the world of sports & entertainment. With this prestige; the Negro will be able to intermarry with the Whites and began a process which will deliver America to our cause."

Brainstorming

This is the demonstration
Crimes against humanity
Have no real re-precautions
Our government
Guilty of pre-meditated genocide
Proofs of a conspiracy
Still exists
Take the risk
Search for truth
Seek to gain
New world order
Not a game
A scary spooky claim
Due to certain altercations
Alienations
Rights deigned, then granted
I've seen the scheme
Erased that "Dream"
Which, encouraged so many
Catch the "Time"
Majority, the minority
Only in numbers
Amplify the mental
Match the "Wits"
Patch the quilt

Create the New Illuminated Bloodlines
Tailgating the blueprint
Left behind footprints
Bilderbergers and the Rockefellers
Rothschild's and the Kennedy's
I got the remedy
We the people
Create the sequel!

In The Midst

SIMULTANEOUS ERRORS
REASON BEING, OUT OF OUR CONTROL
DAILY DECISONS MADE ON "OUR" BEHALF
I DASH
@ THE OPPORTUNITY TO EXPOSE
OPERATION POPULATION DETERIATION
ALL COALS DON'T TURN TO DIAMONDS
LIKE HOOD RATS TO HOUSEWIVES
RIGGED DICE = LIFE
AN I ADD TO THE DIARY
WHERE IS TRUTH BEHIND CONSPIRACY?
I BEGAN TO QUESTION IT ALL
LIKE BRITANY SPEARS DOWN FALL
MAYA ANGELOU'S STILL I RAISE
TAMARA ALLEN'S UN-CLAIMED PRIZE
BEEN WRITING SINCE TEN
LOVE MY PEN, BOWARROWED, OR OWNED
WRITING ON DIRTY NAPKINS AT THE BAR
AS LONG AS WERE HUMAN BEINGS
DICTATORSHIPS REDEAMS
SOCIAL CLASS TAKES THE PLACE OF RASICM
IS IT A BLACK THING, OR IS A PEOPLE THING?
DID YOU KNOW GOLD STOCK IS UP?
(0) ZERO EQUALS BUCK
YOU KNOW . . . $ THE DOLLAR BILL
SHIT, OIL SPILL WAS ONLY AN ADDITON

NOW FORGOTTEN
NEW WORLD ADVISORY
INTERNET SENSOR
SO THEY EDITED THE OBAMA DECEPTION
KNEW IT ALTER YOUR PERCEPTION
BLACK, AND SOLD
DAYS OF OUR LIVES
NOW THEY GOT A SOAP CALLED CLAY
YOU "NIGGAS" WASH THAT SKIN AWAY
WHAT AN ANIMATED PLAY
I DAMN NEAR GIVE UP, TRYING TO KEEP UP
DON'T EVEN KNOW WHO TO TARGET,
BULLSEYE!
3 STRIKES YOU'RE OUT
ANOTHER DROUGHT, D-BOYS SHOUT
WHILE GOVERNMENT ASSISTANCE GOT YOU LAZY
FOOD STAMPS SOLD DAILY
WHAT HUNGRY BABIES?
CHEATING THE SYSTEM, THAT BEATS YOU
TO THINE SELF I ALWAYS STAY TRUE
Philosophizing WITH NO DOCTORATE
COLLEGE RIP OFF, GIRLS STRIP OFF
GUYS GET OFF, NOW THE LIGHTS TURNED OFF
LET'S SEE HOW DO I END, WHEN THERE IS NO BLEND
PEOPLE MEASURE SIN ON LEVELS, BUT THEY ALL THE SAME
THIEF OR ADULTRY
WE ALL STRIVNG TO BE

Trap Musiq

6.7 million Used
1.3 received treatment
So imprison those who serve
What's in demand?
Command, Control, Alt Delete
Quit's the application
If you want to end illegal drug distribution
Legalize
Since beginning of mankind
Folk been getting "High"
Rather it be earth grown mushrooms
Man Made meth
Ecstasy beaming you the moon
So you thought . . . shit
Sex is a Drug
Work is a Drug
Food is a drug
Anything you do excessively
Due to your depression see
Even those happy want the high
Floating while standing still
Rather it be 2 seconds like Crack
Or Hours like a Double Stack Transformer
Zebra print purple & pink power ranger
Consumers the dummies
Government posing like Gumby

All friendly
They floating the shit in
We didn't land on Plymouth Rock!
You heard it before, need I quote
Illegal drug distribution without a tax stamp
All "They" want is they Cut
D-Boys boast and brag 10 a key
Add that six cent on a dollar
Pay the IRS
Greedy Uncle Sam
Green eggs & Ham
You Niggas still eating spam
Bullshit emails received
Just like dime dope sentences
Bleach don't cover blemishes
Damn my Brutha
My King
I know its fast cash
That shit don't last
Can't beat the system that beats you
I know nothing is what it seems
Everything ain't got to be Dope Boy Dreams
Your worth so much more
Get it together OR
Your Business might = RICO

The Jones

How do you?
Sit around,
Thinking so small
Focused on the mall
What you can buy
While, the AMERO is in
Motion
A cashless money system
One further step
In the domination
I been telling you all along
Make it your concern
"out of control"
Doesn't even title this destruction
We have to fight the power
Never know the hour
I must steak my claim

Leave my scent
Like dog's piss on tree's
Caterpillar's slither on leaves
Cat's shedding on the couch
So, let me shed some light

Please join YOUR fight
READ, then PLANT MORE SEEDS,
Tell the next, send a brotha, or a sista
A TEXT, post it on YOUTUBE, or MYSPACE
BLACK PLANET, YOUR OWN POETRY
See the variety

Never know who you inspire
Let's not be mistaken
As . . .
Hardworking consumers
Rocking ED HARLEY, RALPH LAUREN
EDUCATED but still SLEEP
STRONG but still WEAK
READING with no COMPREHENSION
VOTING, and still DYING!

Bloodlines

DISTINCTIVE FEATURES
PIGMENTATION OF MY SKIN
LEADS ME TO DESCRIBE
THE FOLLOWING
PRE-CONCEIVED NOTATIONS OF MY CREED
COLORED
NEGRO
BLACK
AFRO-AMERICAN
AFRICAN AMERICAN
WHICH IS THE PROPER ADDRESS
NO HUMAN IS COLORED
NEGRO IS A DERRIVITIVE OF THE WORD "NIGGER"
BLACK REFERS TO A COLOR
AFRO REFLECTS A HAIR STYLE
AFRICAN COMES FROM AFRICA
SO, WHO AM I?
THE DECENDANT OF SLAVERY
THE DECENDANT OF THE SLAVE MASTER'S LAST NAME
THE DECENDANT OF NEIGHBORING INDIAN TRIBES
SO, WHAT'S THE CLAIM
NOW, THAT'S A SHAME
TO BE SO STRIPPED
YOU CAN'T FIND YOUR OWN ROOTS
BLACK IS WHITE
WHITE IS BLACK

THEY DON'T TEACH YOU THAT
DEEPER THAN THE COLOR OF SKIN
THE WHOLE IDEA
A DISADVANTAGE
TO AMERICAN PEOPLE
STEROTYPES PLACES ON
PEOPLE, PLACES, & THINGS
ALL MISUNDERSTOOD
HEAVEN IS WHITE
HELL IS BLACK
THE WHITE MAN IS TRUSTED
WHILE THE BLACK MAN IS BUSTED
ON TRUMPED UP CHARGES

WAIT A MINUTE!!!!
WE AIN'T
PAINTED, STAINED, DYED, OR VARNISHED
MOORISH SCIENCE TEMPLE OF AMERICA
TEACHES
LOVE, TRUTH, PEACE, FREEDOM, AND JUSTTICE
TRUST THIS
DESENDANTS OF STRIPPED LAST NAMES
YOU ARE THE TURE BLOODLINE OF THE BEGINNING
YOU ARE THE CREED THAT CREATED ALL CREEDS
SO, THEY STOLE, RE-WROTE, THEN RE-VISED
PERFECT DISQUISE
NOW WE ALL CONFUSED, AND RELATED KIN
TRUTH LIVES AROUND THE CORNER
SEARCH TO FIND . . .

One Third Percent

We jumped them
Bumped stat's out the way
Protocols of Zion
Saved the day
Sports & Entertainment
Umbrella for the hood
Chronology dates back
So called—Freedmen of the south
Breed for extensive task
Running, hiding, marching, fasting for freedom
Centuries marked 1mile . . .
Faith in "Jesus", elapsed time
The sequel is now
We deliver the WOW
Social Mobility is mutable
The Struggle crippled, but rippled
The Domino Effect
CEO'S, and MVP'S,
Listen & watch
On MP3'S, and DVD'S

Still working hard to get In-House
Do you recall him, the house—"Negro"
This date in time, the "Hood Figure"
Either way it goes
Classification Code: Identity Crisis
The many of that do succeed
Get on the first thing smoking
Out the hood, to a gated community
Giving charity to overseas, when home is diseased
Momz always said
Charity starts @ Home
Hurricane
Katrina affected us all
Turning on the news, seeing my reflection
Receiving nothing but rejection
Until Ophra
Brought her own damn cameras
Zooming in on the displaced refugees
Oooh la la
Remember the Fugees?
How can it be, who could flee
To a foreign country!

Maize

They watching you from, space threw your own T.V.
Via satellite, better yet, CABLEVISON
Did you give permission?
Not so clear as high definition
Masked conspiracies
Contradiction in Theology
What's friendship without apology?
Running game through Psychology
Wish I could master Numerology
Ancients hand spinned pottery
Too much Technology
So, we hardly use our brains
2 second delay
Listen to what I say
Don't get caught in the hype
Please let's go on strike
Don't buy gas
We can car pool, ride the bus, ride the train,
Subway
Last, but not least ride a bike
Never safe enough to hitch hike
Catch the scenario
Synchronized networking
Put you're my space to some real use

I've meet many great thinkers
Due to the World Wide Web
Why not make them dread
The creation of this "On-Line Portal"
We can all collab together, and go postal
In a phenomenal, positive way
The shouting echo's "Wake Up!"
Remember College Daze?
Message still the same
Let's fight the power, before we all get
Devoured!!

ENTRANCES/EXITS

Nana Rose

Hey NaNa
I missed you today
"Lil Old Lady"
Just cause you use to call me
"Lil Old Girl"
I'll paddle your behind!
You better listen, and Mind
Your elders, for your days will be long
Those words still strong
Your voice in my head
Being angry use to be easier,
Cause I'd just come chat with you
All the things you said, so true
Such a homely feeling, sitting on your couch
I'd just lie back, and slouch
Eventually to fall asleep
You'd just sit there knitting, and watching
As soon as I'd awake
There be a nice hot plate
And,
Every Birthday for 25years
I received a card, 5bucks, & homemade Cherry Cheesecake
Oh, do I miss those day's
When I'd call you and say, Nana
What you doing today?
You would say....Old Author steady bothering me
But, a rose stands strong, and sturdy
Your white hair, combed, and tightly curled
So, short you were
I remember to the tee

The only Grandma that really loved me
A Rose, is still a Rose
Even though not physical to the eye
Your presence is sincerely missed
So is your Kiss.
Love you Nana, I miss you

DEDICATED TO MY GRANDMOTHER

ROSA LEE WASHINGTON

NOVEMBER 11 1916- OCTOBER 30, 2005

Calling From the Sky

God say's He will come
'Like a thief in the night'
That has to be quite right
Cause I'm lost
Left in the dark
Without a candle
Or, a torch
Can't think straight
Starring at you picture
Calling your phone
Just to hear your voice
I have no Choice
What is self-worth
Without you?
The reason I listen to sad music
The answer to future happiness
The thought that brightened my day
Saddened my smile
The person that made me complete,
And, left alone.

From with In

Tears, Tears, Tears
Years, Years, Years
Pain, Pain, Pain,
Delays, Delays, Delays
Faith, Faith, Faith,
Try, Try, Try
Why? Why? Why?

Am I clouded in this
Funky molded cabbage
Odor
Asking Satan to move over
Like a game of "Red Rover, Red Rover"
Living in Sin
Expecting to win

Such a battle with-in
I die, and then awake
At times
Depends on my frame of mind
Maybe, I seem insane

Dead on arrival
What I'm thinking most of the time
My Botha's aren't getting a fair chance at
1/3 of life's glance

Before Murdered
So, The Colbert show goes on reporting political news
While the "Hood" sing's the Blues

Like Fiends, smoking away dreams
The suit in the casket
So Fresh, and So Clean
Soul already Beamed
Either, they don't know it
Or they don't show it
Doe Boy quoted
I'm just saying to many lives, getting shorted.

In Memorie Of Shawn Bell

The journey set before my feet
No telling who I meet
Greet to seek
Seek to gain
Media leaked Watergate scandal
Katrina money a scam
Weighing less than .5grams
On the scale
Law's escape bail
After 50 shot's fired
VOICES GET HIRED
No excuse for the loss
Who pays the cost, not the Boss
"niggas" just floss
Don't raise hell
Souls sold to the Money well
Our future for sale?

Otis

Same Place, different time
We been doing this so long
All of us know how to stay strong
The preacher might say
Wipe those tears away
God don't make no mistakes!
This is all understood
Now, let's discuss this hood
Black on black crime
Another brother serving time
When will in all go in sync
We have lost so many
To violence in the street
"LiL Boo" was too young to be gone
It will be hard for many
To say Goodbye
Like Sty's to Eyes
Passing on by
And in that Rose bed
Your roots were snatched
The story ends so damn cold
Never know what life unfolds
Your soul has made its passage
That bright beautiful smile
Is far from ever being forgotten
As this stanza comes to an end
Let's all digest that a new life begins

Obituary of Dub-K

THE REAL RECOGNIZE
THE REAL
THEY PART THE UNIVERSE 1ST
AN EMPTY VERSE
OR
A CAVE W/O AN ECHO
IS
LIFE W/O LOVE

FRIENDSHIP OR SOULMATE
FAMILY OR FOE
THE HEART IS AT STEAK
WHEN, EVER GIVEN A BREAK

A STAKE THROUGH THE HEART
NOT ONLY KILLS VAMPIRES
BUT, THE HEADS OF EMPIRES
THE ILLS OF THE UNIVERSE
LET'S TRY TO CONVERSE, A SECOND

WHY, ASK WHY?
ONLY TO BE TOLD A LIE
ONE WING BIRDS DON'T FLY
SO, LET'S HEAL

PROLIFERATE

IN UNITY
PROTECT OUR COMMUNITIES
WROTE TOO MANY ELEGY'S
BROTHA'S GUNED DOWN

A CONSIDERED SMALL TOWN
FULL OF GHOST
TO MANY EXPERIENCED THE LOSS
COURT TRAILS
REALITY A DENAIL

TESTIMONY AFTER TESTIMONY
NO MATRIMONY
JUST GORY PICTURES OF YOUR DEAD BODY
BLOODY CLOTHES
PLAY BY PLAY OF YOUR LAST BREATH
ALL DESCRIBED BY TOTAL STRANGERS
I'LL NEVER FORGET
I WILL NOT WISH IT UP ON MY WORST ENIMIE
DEATH, OR 24YR LIFE SENTENCE
WHAT FORGIVANCE, NEVER TO BE OBTAINED
ONE MORE BAD MEMORIE GAINED

Simba

Try to find the words
To describe my emotions
Create a potion
To digest dissolution
Soon as I swallow
Reality
There is more brutality
Hypothetically speaking
Can I have a friend?
To never cry a river for
Got the shivers
Chills ran down my spine
Couldn't blame it on a drive by shooting
12 minutes of Oxygen
Lost to the brain
Beaten by a cane
Overdose of cocaine
For those things mostly happen to humans
I was so lucky
To be loved by my puppy
Until a car, ran him over
Now, I can't stay sober!

*I remember when I wrote this 11:42pm Jan 27 2005, my Professor at Wichita State University had given a poetry writing assignment. He graded this poem as unclear, so let me explain this one. I had lost several friends due to several different types of murders before my Puppy named Simba died, so I was simply saying I was sick of grieving!

Goodbye

As I stand beside you bedside
Starring in your eyes, I wonder
What's going on inside
Your body is in Convolutions,
And your eyes open wide

We all stand around awaiting our turn
To come in your room
Give comforting words
I grab your hand, and wish hard
Wondering
Are you coming with me, or going with him?

Family and friends eyes pocket full of tears
Visitation has ceased
Vegetable state
Our prayers are sent, will they return?
Your eyes respond to all unanswered questions
Your not coming with us, you're going with him

Through God all things are possible
Faith in prayer brings about change

I guess in your case it was meant
For you to say Good-Bye

R.I.P
Michael "Girdy" Calhoun
July 4th 1979 - Feb 16 2001

Catching Up

The termination of Biological functions
Due to a hand gun
is a hard pill to swallow
Tellus, what can I say?
But, that
many still can't turn that page
Your Mother finds it hard
Even looking at your picture
She stays focused on her scriptures
Your brother is taking it, day by day
And, All of your true friends
Never strayed away
You have a Niece & a nephew now
You'd be so proud
Your favorite "Sweet Pea" just graduated college
I know you'd be so elated
It's been a long 6 years
The fear of what's next
Keeps me stressed
So, I try and Cherish those dear
Never know when the end, is near
Love is pain (tattooed it after your death)
Rather your a Mother
Brother, Lover, Family Member, or Friend
Were all Blessed, yet Cursed
With Life & Death

Tamara T. Allen

The same day is never confirmed
You are certainly loved, and Most definitely missed
To you I blow, this invisible Kiss
Happy Birthday Friend
One day we will meet again!

J.J.C.

Wounds just don't heal

Sometimes

Even when I neel, and Pray

I don't understand

Couldn't **YOU** *have had a 2nd chance?*

I wanted another glance

All I got, was confirmation, Then cremation . . .

Remembering it All

DOES ANYONE KNOW THE ENERGY IT TAKES TO LOVE,
WITHOUT DESIRE FOR RECOGNITION?

TO CLOSE A CHAPTER, WITH NO REAL UNDERSTANDING

TO SAY GOOD-BYE, NOT GOODNIGHT?

Especially when you're not ready to face another battle

FIRST IT WAS . . .
"JR" Lionel K Smith
THEN IT WAS . . .
"BIG GIRDY" Michael Calhoun
THEN IT WAS . . .
"KING LUV" Marcus Cox
THEN IT WAS . . .
TELLUS JEROME COLVIN
THEN IT WAS . . .
CHRISTOPHER SPAIN-BEY

The attempt to take on the next person's burdens,
    maybe not to take them on
Just to try and understand, and make life a little less stressful
See, I knew you were hurting
See, I knew you wasn't strong
See, I knew just when to speak, when to update you on the trail

When to smile with you, and when it was okay to cry around you

I had to stay strong, not just for me, but mostly for you
How could I be weak, when that would just push you away?

Nobody could ever understand or compare to your loss
So that's why I ask . . .

DOES ANYONE KNOW THE ENERGY IT TAKES TO LOVE,
WITHOUT DESIRE FOR RECOGNITION?

Years later, I'd say many that I stood strong for, don't even see

BLABBING TO MY SISTA'S!

99.9%

BLINK TWICE, YOU MISSED
INVISIBLE KISS
LOOKED YOU IN THE EYE
ASSUME THE REST
AT YOUR BEST, YOU WON'T CATCH
BUTTERFLY'S ROAM THE SKY
TOUR THE UNIVERSE, COME BACK, AND CONVERSATE

FIX YOUR PLATE, WASH YOUR CLOTHES, THEN EXPOSE,
LOVE WON'T ROT MY COT

PUT FLEE'S IN MY BED, RELEASE MY SOUL
BODY EMPTY, FULL OF SYMPATHY,
PATHETIC SOAP OPRA
WAITING ON A 'Nigga" TO COP YA
A DIRTY BLOOD DIAMOND
DROP TO HIS KNEE, BEG A SISTA PLEASE
I IPRESENT YOU THIS DISEASE
WITHOUT KNOWING . . . YOU'VE BEEN SNORING
DROWLING AT THE MOUTH, HE BIG DOWN SOUTH
BRAGGED TO YA GIRLS, NOW THEY INFECTED. ☹

Sleeping Beauty

What's Beauty?

Long Hair, Light Skin, Thick, Round Ass

What about me,

Dark skinned, Nappy Hair, Slender, Flat Ass

Well Damn, I can't get a shot out

A salute

A damn tribute

References constantly made to Trina

All the Geneva Divas

Sista's Don't get me wrong, I ain't hating

I'm Just doing my Usual debating

Preferences are okay, but must we be divided in this way

The slave master rapped your Great, Great, Great Grandmother

She birthed "Light Skin"

It is always the darkest Brother

Talking this yippy yappy, requesting that 1B Yacky

Wanting you to wiggle, and do the laffy taffy

Ideal of beauty Baffling

I know, I know, It's entertainment

But, Let's be fair

All black women don't grow luxurious long hair

We don't all have "Big Booty Judy" asses for display

Our curvatious figures are no doubt a great inheritance

But, there is more for you to see

Brothas, when you describe me

Be rich in content, descriptive in your imagery

Put a 10 on my swagg

Don't limit me to light skin, long hair, thick, round ass

I come in all shapes, sizes, colors, and forms

It ain't what's between my legs, it's what's in my head!

Love

EVERY WOMAN
CAN'T HANDLE THE ILLUSION
STAGED CHEMESTRY
ALL WHILE KNOWING HIS HISTORY
LOVE A COMPLEX MYSTERY
BLINDING YOU, ALTHOUGH YOU HAVE PERFECT SIGHT
ONE DAY HE JUST MIGHT
CHANGE,
MAINTAIN ROCKY SHORES
BUT, THERE ARE SO MANY DAMN WHORES!
AT SAME TIME
SO MANY, DECIENT, AVAILABLE, BEAUTIFUL WOMEN
HE NEVER HAS TO CHOOSE
WHILE SO MANY LOOSE THEIR SELVES
NOT EVEN ACTING IN TRUE CHARACTER
SUCH A DEADLY, DRAMATIC GAME
SOME WOMEN ARE NOT ASHAMED
TO ACT OUT, SCREAM, SHOUT,
SNICKER BARS
IN YOUR GAS TANK
AS MISS SULLIVAN SAID
"I BUST THE WINDOWS OUT YOUR CAR"
SOMETIMES THOSE DAMN LIES GO TO DAMN FAR
FOR A WOMAN TO DIGEST
GET IT WO-MAN
PARTIAL VERSION OF YOU
WELL I SAY

THIS WOMAN CAN HANDLE IT
ALL THE BETRAYLE, HURT, AND PAIN
IS NOW MY GAIN, STRONGER FOR THE NEXT
LOVE A NEVER ENDING CONQUEST
PEOPLE SPEND A LIFE TIME
IN SEARCH OF A SPOUSAL UNIT
SOMEONE TO AGE WITH THREW THE MILLENIUMS
HOWEVER ALL MOST PEOPLE WANT TO DO IS "cuM"
EXPLICT WORD FOR ORGASIM
BETTER YET SARCASIM
DON'T THINK IM BITTER FOR WHAT I'M ABOUT TO SAY
SEX IS OVERATED, WHEN IT'S A DUMMY STAGE
PEOPLE PRETENDING, TRYING TO STAGE A FAMILY ENDING
THAT BEGAN WITH NO TRUE INTREST
LADIES I'M GIVING YOU THE GAME
SHIT YOU TIRED OF BEING HURT
WELL THEN CONVERT, CLOSE YOUR LEGS
LET HIM BEG
GET TO KNOW YOUR MATE
MAYBE YOU WON'T BE SURPRISED BY THE FATE
EVEN WHEN YOU DO IT THE RIGHT WAY
KNOW THAT IT STILL MIGHT NOT LAST
PLAY YOUR TRUEST CHARACTER
IN THE END, IT WILL ALL REGISTER
TO MANY IT DOESN'T,
SO THEY KILLED THEIR MAIT, AND THEN THEMSELVES,
SOME CASES EVEN THE KIDS,
LOVE IS A STRONG, SERIOUS, SENSITIVE EMOTION
IF NOT HANDLED WITH CARE, PLEASE BEWARE!
BUT, MOST OF YOU DON'T CARE
SO, IM WRITING THIS FOR YOU
WATCH OUT, PAY ATTENTION TO WARNING SIGNS
REMEMBER LORENA BOBBET, NO MORE COMMENTS!

To My Fellow Ladies!!!!!

WHO CARE'S IF I'M PRETTY
WHO CARE'S IF I'M NOT
THIS BODY WILL ROT
LIFE SENTENCES ON COT'S
DALMATIONS WITHOUT SPOT'S
A LIFE WITHOUT A MIRROR
A PETITE FIGURE
A ROUND ASS
THEY CALL IT HOUR GLASS
SO, GIRLS DIET FAST
PUSH-UP'S, SIT-UP'S, CRUNCHES
BUNCHES OF OAT'S
HOLLYWOOD DEVOTION
GOT THROATS IN TIOLETS
SILOUTTES SIMULAR TO THOSE
NEGATIVE PICTURES CAPTURED IN AFRICA
BUT, AIN'T NO FLY'S & RICE LYING AROUND
AND, THAT A SHAME
TO STARVE BY CHOICE, WHILE OTHER'S FORCED
A SIMPLE SICKNESS DIAGNOSED
SELF-ESTEEM THE CURE

My Uterus

The Right to life, right to strife
Who really has the choice?
Besides the un-born baby
Does it really matter?
A rape victim,
A child hit by a drunk driver
A father slaughtered at war
Nobody was given the choice
They just heard that voice
Calling them to the heavens
Pro-Life, or Pro-Choice
Bigger worries, Heavy stress
Major attention for individual decisions
Brings double standards
Currency say's "In one God we Trust"
The age of accountability
Proves is for once, and for all
Let God do his job for us All
I stand Pro-Choice
Wrong, or right
No one escapes the wrath
So, let the debate pass

Wo-Man

What is the Probability?
A sista will not
Become a statistic
Of
Abortion
Teen age Pregnancy
Single parenthood
Rape
Domestic violence

Forced to silence
Crimes of men
Who can we depend on?
To defend us
Most brothas we can't trust
That's the percentage I made
The man that wanted to take what was not his
Tripped up the stairs
Trying to get away

Damn near want to give Adam is rib back!

Wondering why God didn't
Make us as strong
So we can really protect ourselves
Hot Grit's scold's skin

Burning lies from the Begin-ING
Eve sinning
Created the worlds beginning
A man's perception

Eternal deception
Gender Inferiority
A man, a Wo-man
He can do, but I can't
Or
I'm judged!
Society's Double Standards
Bastard babies
Born out of wedlock
Old fashion views
Just like
Genesis scriptures

ILLUSTRATIONS OF
MY SOUL

Feb262004

My heart yanked from my body
Don't want to party
Don't want to smile
Happiness no longer dwells here

I know you don't want me to cry

But, I wonder why
You know how much I love you
Never could stop
Dwelling over our union

Our soul ties

You were my soul mate
I wish our souls
Would have left this earth
At the same time

Not like; Romeo & Juliet

Suicide
Leads straight to hell
I mean

In death together
You and I
Like birds fly
Existing in harmony
What should I fear?
The pain of shots fired
Tearing through flesh
Is only temporary
The pain of loosing you lasts a lifetime

Community Foreplay

Where Is my equalibruim
Vitiamans from centruim
Cant donate enough energy
So called friends that lack chemistry
THE RISE & FALL SITCOM
THEN . . . The Repeated Epidsodes
Last Season, only creates a new season
When is it just over
Is there a real Casanova?
Maybe there is just Yoga, and CONDOMS 2 GO
Back to the Re-Run
The dating game is a shame
So the married ones thinking the grass
Is greener on the other side
STAY ON YOUR SURF & RIDE!

Mi Amor

I'm In love
With a beautiful
Painting
It just hangs on the wall
And, all I can do is Stare
A glance, just gets me by
Just imagine, so little gets me high
I mean, I can never have this beautiful painting
So, now I'm just thinking
How dumb can I be
Leaving my heart hanging form a tree
Gossip Buzzing like bees
This painting is not authentic, they say
My mind just drifts away
I knew I'd never have it anyway
I still slipped, and fell
Fake ass love spell
I understand you so well
you don't even know that my heart dwells
In the shadows of you
I play it off, playing my position
As a simple bidder at the Art Gallery

Just Thinking

When did we loose it all
I'm speaking on love
like twin doves
better yet two black gloves
I remember being young
like "Tim & Kim"
like 'Shay & Jamaal"
then shrinking so small
settling for less
no finesse from caress
steaming baths' with baby oil
can't sooth
my broken heart
my love dead & gone
murdered, departured
and, yes I tried again
wrong choice
his friend
we mourned the same loss
attended the same murder trail'
I'm in no denial
no fronts for Facebook
like all you married crooks
pretending to be
I'M just me
another Long Island

deep breath . . .
I miss you
"never knew what a friendship was
never knew how to really love"
quote by Erykah Badu
feeling so blue
remembering when I first met you
feels like I am trespassing
never wanted to step on ones toes
funny how positions change
like the contents re-arranged
last names changed
time aged
feelings still the same

The Duality of Love

The most stimulating love
Is innocent . . .
Bright as florescent colors
That smell of **authenticity**
Serenading the air
The imagery of this Love
Is way too far fetched for explanations
It just simply exists
Soaking up space
Until forced intervention
The "tie" that binds
Nature of humanity
Creates lovatious fantasy's
Which manifest reality
Then, intensity occurs

A new love surges
Like electric currents
Causing heart failure
And then . . .
You fall in Love

The Duality of Love
Represents Persistence . . .

The most refreshing Love

Is that of lust . . .
Physical attraction
The animal instinct with in
It technically isn't love, but in most cases
Ends in love,
Which represents **convenience**
To Love for these reasons
Is sacrifice of the soul
Gratification of the flesh

Who knows best
Other, than those in quest for love
Experimentation brings knowledge
YOU live, and THEN you LEARN

The Duality of Love

The Shred

WATCH OUT
KARAMATIC CONSEQUENCES
ROUGH TO COPE
TO KNOW YOU, PLAYED PART
THEN, THINGS FELL APART
ALL KNOWN FROM THE START
CATEPILLARS FORM INTO BUTTERFLY'S
WHEN YOU CATCH THEM
TRAP THEM IN A JAR
ENJOY THE BEAUTY FROM AFAR
I CAUGHT YOU, CAN'T TRAP YOU
CAN'T TRIP, TAKE A TIP
THIS A SHORT CLIP
SOMEONE ELES MOVIE
I JUST ADDED TO THE SCANDEL
NOW, I CAN'T HANDLE
WHAT WAS ALWAYS KNOWN
THIS IS YOUR MISSON
ALL ALONE, I CAN'T COME ALONG!

Courting

Does time tell?
The fate or outcome
The more you wait
The less you can take

Share, Share, Share
That is all I run into
Go about it the right way
And, still have to play

One Minute, One night
Six Months, Wedding Night
It doesn't matter
Things will change

Soon there after
You've given up
All precious goods
Truth comes ashore

He's not ready
He can't be steady
Stuck in a bad situation
Caught up in relations

Hoping relations
Turn to a relationship
Is your biggest downfall
So, don't fall!

For that same tired game
Gain the fame
Win the score
You deserve more

Never settle for less
Put him to the test
Your offer is the best
Come with me, or GO AWAY!

Four Letter Word

ALL THAT IT IS . . .

ALL THAT IS NOT . . .

ALL THAT IT CAN BE . . .

ALL THAT IT SHOULD HAVE BEEN . . .

ETERNITY IT CAN LAST . . .

IN SECONDS, NOW THE PAST . . .

HOW MANY TIMES YOU CAN FIND IT . . .

HOW MANY TIMES YOU RENEW IT . . .

HOW TIMES WILL YOU LOOSE IT . . .

BEFORE YOU REALLY SEE IT, UNDERSTAND IT,
& RESPECT IT . . .

LOVE

Empty

Who is he, he that is equal to me?
And where might he lay, is it where I may stay
Such a fun game to play, called find your soul mate
Fuck around get stood up on the first date
And to avoid games, maybe the marriage should be arranged
Would that change the game?
It least you know he ready,
But my name is not Susan
So I be losing, these chicks be choosing,
However I'm waiting to get chosen!
Old skool some may say, either way love is delayed!

The Past

Threw my heart in the river,
Floated right back,
Not a compository safe to save my face,
I embrace, no room for misplaced "feelings",
Images,
Scrimmages,
Opposition in the team,
Practices don't always make for perfect!
Depends on the subject,
Destiny, got the best of me,
So I am scheming my departure,
Life passes by fast,
Turn your back, slip fall in a crack,
Deep down under,
I need a plunger from being sunk-in
Sharing the "bunk bed"
Known
The revolving penis
Don't rhyme with genius!
Acts without discression supplements depression,
Learned another lesson.
How did I get here? Struck by a spear, fake ass cupid, aren't I stupid!

Misapprehension

Just to say, I love you
Is so simple
Everyone doesn't have dimples
Slip you foot in the shoe

It fits, so wear it
The circumference of the pie
A perfect measure for un-seen eyes
Don't want to spare, it

Never mind, revolving shadows of secrecy
Intimacy influenced by hands of lust
Evidence of no trust
Exceptions made for acts of true sincerity

My mind badgers, thee, or he
Who my soul has chosen
My beloved has not arisen
How could this be?

Another love, projected forever unable to see
With sight of grief
He gave me relief
Like a summer breeze from a tree

I feel beneath, thee
A marry Magdalene
I can only imagine
What others would say, knowing I feel this way?

WEB OF DECEPTION

Religious Controversy

REAL, OR FAKE?
RELIGON BRINGS HOPE
WITHOUT KNOWLEDGE OF FAITH
A BRIGHTER DAY
THIS TOO SHALL PASS
GOD DON'T PUT NUTHING ON YOU THAT YOU CAN'BEAR
RELIGIOUS QUOTES OF COMFORT
I WON'T FURTHER DISTORT MY VISION
WITH QUESTION AFTER QUESTION
HOLY GRAIL, TRUE BLOODLINE OF CHRIST
VIRGIN MARY
DEBATABLE ALL DAY
IF THERE WERE NO RED PRINT
SAVAGES WOULD SHREAD US ALL
KUDOS TO THE GENIUS
THAT HAS TRICKED US ALL!

Demonstrate My Sista!

Egyptian Mythology quadruplized
Greeks, Romans, and Christians
Plagiarized, inserted a few words
Renamed prophets, teachers, and seer's
Revised law's for the land
Tall tails, jezebel's stoned for adultery
Duplicated Crucifixions, false predictions
Contradicting parables
Old testament vs. New
Was Jesus really a Jew?
I hope not, check out the irony
6million murdered, now, enslave us all
International Bankers, finance credit, so we thankful
Let's try and be watchful
How tasty is a pot of veggie stew?
Without the beef, naked
Call it biblical manipulation
Kept the slaves in tact, on they knees, praying
Does prayer work, or does time keep advancing
We don't need slaves in the field, shackles to tie us down
How about a micro-chip, or an RFID
Creates a great variety
Used to control terrorism
Buy food, gas, water, electric
Similar to a GPS tracker, so your always safe

Your killer caught on tape
Ain't this GREAT!
Fake ass solution, fake ass drama
Real drama consist of pissed off baby's mama's
Who, do it all own their own
Right back,
A government that doesn't even own it's self, own's you
Controls your brain
News & Media blinds
No Osama Bin Laden
Just Barrack Obama making history
I'm steady solving this mystery
My thoughts jump, SO KEEP UP . . .

Stay tuned, while I explain The Sun & The Moon
It was never the world ending, but a new phase beginning
Like my period on the 1st of every month
This earth circulates on it's axis
Search the Forbidden, astrology
You will understand repetition
Pre-historic animals, now extinct, new species born
Who use to know, when it snowed
Now, Doppler radar, so take shelter
The Sun & Moon destroys, then Restores
Think about Jesus, he represents the same
Even those praised before him
Who needs religion to define right, from wrong?
Religion is for social control, and works in our favor
Only when truth is known
When, you move past that
Our most important venture, protecting our future
Surviving through the ages, with Freedom
Never accomplished before, so get ready for War.

The End

Last of the Poets . . . Please!
Literary warrior undiscovered
A language that proceeds the future
Druids wrote on trees
Feel the breeze
From thought's written on paper
Which don't get grades, scores, or ratings
Just belligerent statements
Views of dates & time
Un-necessary to always rhyme

Inspire a little, then what
So what?
Guess what?
But, then what
Okay I'm ready
Already contemplated
Life with no loss, no floss
Only gloss on glass windows
Sweeky clean

Now, that vision is clear
After time expires
The same thing will take place
remember Noah's Ark?

The Ice Age
This earth will revolve
Re-invent it's identity
Just as many of us do DAILY!

Please Let Me In!

SHOULD HAVE BEEN
COULD HAVE BEEN
DOESN'T MATTER

Life don't hand you a platter
Steak, Shrimp, and Eggs
I begg
For mercy

Why, curse me
Charge a service fee
To the gates of Heaven?

Life

Life's cup always half empty
Take the Agnostic approach
Questions of the unknown answered simply
No more reliance on the pull-pit coach

Observations taken without reference of theory
Makes for an open state of mind
Ye, for the path of truth long and eerie
Let's go back in time, press rewind

Knowledge so eminent never to be written
Forbidden fruits and treasures
Trace the steps of a kitten
Impossible to gather this measure

Using allegory lines with common sense
Educating yourself is only self-defense!

Revelation

One thousand tons weights my shoulders
My eyes are growing colder
I yearn for understanding
Days are gloomy, nights pitch dark
Four thousand darts plunged into my heart

Death as a sense of peace
Only comes though eternal life
Eternal life is only given
Through God
If you could have it
Would you take it?

Life is full of struggle
Struggle is pain
Future full of black rain
Choking on marijuana
Drunken with liquor
Escapes the pressure

The end is near
Bigger things to fear
Every knee shall bow
Every eye shall confess
Will you pass the test?
Do you care where you soul rests?

SPEAKING TO MY PEOPLES

Checking You Brothers!

Who was Adam, Without Eve
Martin Luther King; Without Coretta Scott
A broke Nigga, without a "cut buddy"
A trap star, without a "down ass bitch"
A pimp, without a "HOE"
President Bush, Without Condoleezza Rice!

Get it?
Ain't NO coinsidence
We are your equivalent
Your confident, your perfect friend
Reflection of you
So, why the disrespect!
VERBAL ABUSE
EMOTIONAL ABUSE
PHYSICAL ASSULT
RAPE
ABANDOMENT

How many "homeboy's" raise your seeds
Take your dope cases
stand by your side, cover up your lies
give you their last dollar
last breath
see . . . we die giving birth

You Brotha's should be ashamed
Your "Mind Frame"
Fuck a Hoe, Fuck a Bitch, Come suck my Dick

But, you steady taking advantage
of a Sista
Fuck ya homeboy, then
some of you do anyway (LOL!)
Be a Fag
Come correct, or don't "CUM"
It's 8 to 1 in many places

If the head is sleep
Then the body "num"
Brotha's sleep walking fresh in "J's"
Stiletto's in the shadow
King's arise, set the stage
You got 8 QUEEN'S waiting!

Can you take care of them all?
Then don't touch
Solomon housed all his hoe's
You Brotha's got it all wrong
Sista's throw away ya thong's
Stand for something
We make it harder, for each other

Cool with being the "OTHER"
Not pressing charges, when Raped
Letting him stay, when the rent ain't paid
Ain't helping with the Baby, but still Sexing
Turning against your friends & family
Cause he beating you to sleep, you too embarrassed to tell

Bills left in your name
At the clinic diagnosed with AIDS

New Phase

PEACE KING, LET'S BE ONE

STRENGTHEN OUR RACE

PLOT OUR FUTURE

OUR TAKEOVER

POEM OVER

Contradiction—The Slave Conspire

LONG SINCE THE DAYS OF COTTON CULTIVATION
THE NEGRO REVELATION
THE YOUNG, OLD, and RESTLESS
HUMPED OVER, BLOODY HANDS
ACCEPTING DEMANDS
SO HE, POPPED THE CHERRY
FATHERED A BABY
BRANDED OUR FUTURE, WITH, HIS LAST NAME
FAIR SKINNED, NOW WE ALL BLEND
WITH A CHOOSEN FEW
MANY DON'T KNOW WHAT TO DO?, WHO TO BE?
DUE TO THESE METHODS
UNIFICATION WAS ACCOMPLISHED
IN CENTURIES OF FURY, BLOODSHEED
CIVIL RIGHTS ACTIVIST FOUND DEAD!
"WHITE ABOLITIONIST", HELPED A NEGRO OUT
WE CAN'T TAKE ALL THE CLOUT
FOR THE FREEDOM OF THE SEAS
GOODLUCK FROM "BLACK EYE PEAS"

Microphone Ck

I'M DONE TELLING YALL
EAR'S AIN'T RECEPTIVE
FUTURE PROJECTED
OVERBOARD IS NOT PRESENT
SHIT, AIN'T PLESANT
WE PESANTS
LIVING BY PERMITS, NO TRACE OF DESENDANTS
BRACE'S STRAIGTEN TEETH
PAIN REVEAL GRIEF
BREAD RISES FROM YEAST, WHY NOT FEAST?
ROAST, CARROTS, POTATOES & GREENS . . .
LIMA BEANS NASTY, LIKE LIES FROM MOM & DAD
PREP'S WEAR PLAIDS, NEVER FIT FAD'S
MISSION SAD, ZOMBIES ROAM, GOVERNMENT CLONES
FOOD WE DIGESTING
MY PEN IMPRESSIVE
YOU GOT SUGGESTIONS, EXPRESS THEM!

The Stat Factor

A.I.D.S EPIDEMIC

WHAT A GIMICK

PERCENTAGE RATES

HEIGHTENED BY BLACKS

LAYING ON THIER BACKS

WITH NO CONTRACEPTION

SOME WITH NO PERCEPTION

OF REALITY IN TRUE SENSE

MENTALLY SLEEP

SUBJECT MATTER

TOO DEEP

I SNEAK W/ MESSAGES

ON THE TABLE

BROTHA'S & SISTA'S

FROM ROYAL BLOODLINES

MAKE SURE THE SUN SHINES

DON'T BE LEFT BEHIND

YOU'RE NOT THE HEIGHT OF ALL CRIMES

STATISTICS THAT LACK CIVILIZATION

FIVE CIVILIZED TRIBES

GOVERNMENT OFFERS BRIBES

GREAT MINDS SELL SOULS

TO THE "SALAD BOWL"

"MELTING POT"

I SMOK POT

PUT' S ME ON THINKING LEVEL

MUST DEFEAT THE DEVIL

THAT HIGHER LEVEL

HIERACHEY

THAT CONTROLLS US ALL

TAKE THE DOWNFALL

INNOCENT CIVILIANS

LIVES UN-SPAIRED

DONATED TO WAR

GIVE ME LIBERTY, OR GIVE ME DEATH

WHAT A CONQUEST

TO DO MY BEST

INFORMING

CONCERNING

DISFORMING CONSITUTIONAL RIGHTS

FILL ME WITH FRIEGHT

ASSINATION OF MY SIGHT

GOT TO STAY DOWN

KEEP WEARING MY CROWN

TRUE QUEEN

DEDICATED TO YOU

SO, PLEASE LISTEN

READ MY POETRY

Invest To Gain

Tangled webs we thread
Nappy like dreads
The feeling of after math
Even the steamiest bath
Won't cloudy the scheme
Similarities in disparity of men
When there's blood on the streets
Collect cash . . .
Old quote, revised meaning
Jeezy dreaming came true
Once in a billion, everyone can't be a Hilton
Old money, beat's new money
Generational cash lasts
A reputation is tied
Not what you know, but who?
Remember that, and then take a nap
Rest a little, life bitter
Like sour fruit,
I'm so cute, cause I know the truth!

Turn Me Up!

EVERY SECOND COUNTS
LIKE VOTES
I TRY & HAVE HOPE
MY FOLKS CATCH MY DRIFT
TAKE NOTES, INQUIRE, DESIRE
TO KNOW TRUTH
FIGHT THE FORCE
STAR WARS, LIFE CHORES
THE GLORY AIN'T CLAIMED
SHINE OFF SMALL FAME
PICTURES IN FRAMES
MINDS IN CHAIN'S
BODIES BEHIND BARS
SCARS FADE WITH COCCA BUTTER
THOUGHTS CLUTTERED
SO, I RELEASE TENSION
WITH MY PEN, AGAIN & AGAIN
I SCREAM ALOUD
TRY & GATHER CROWDS
THINKING OUT LOUD DON'T REACH OUT
NEED A MIC SO I CAN SHOUT!
TURN THE VOLUME UP, STILL DON'T LISTEN!

The Dopest

Every color of the rainbow
Set out, to taint
Your natural sense
Rational state of mind
Who knew?
A beautiful flower
Grown in the summer
Could be dried
Soaked in toxins
Chemically transferred
To power substance
Injected into society
Major factor
Of the G.N.P
There is one in every family
Caught in the spell
Of poison
Look at the world
Around you
Taking advantage
Of the drug, and the addiction
Quick way to fast money
A window of opportunity
Projected to turn positive

The Master of Evil debts
Always chooses the right vessels
To mend the seams
End all dreams!!

Midnight Blue

THE LAST OF THE DYING BREED
KNOWLEDGE TO FEED
THE YOUTH
AGE OF EXPIRATION APPROACHES
LEFT TO THE WORDS OF TEXT BOOKS

THE NEXT CROOK
SHOULD EXPLOIT TRUTH
INSTEAD OF PITFALLS
OF THE MIGHTY GHETTO
POLARIZED DOPE SELLING

EVIDENCE COMPELLING
UN-PROSECUTED
BUT, ATTRIBUTED
TO CLEVERNESS
TO SURVIVE THE GAME
GLORIFIED
TO KEEP MANY SLEEP
YEARNING FOR ICE
THING'S NICE
NEVER HAD BEFORE
YEAH, I LIKE THEM BOYS
BOY'S WHO BE GRILLIN'
BUT, I REALLY LIKE THEM BOYS
WHO B' CHILLIN

PLANNIN WHAT'S NEXT
WANNA WRITE CHECKS
NOT, JUST CASH THEM
KEEP CALCULATING
INSTEAD OF RE-COPIN
FALL OFF—TRY AGAIN
POSSIBLY END UP
LYING IN A GRAVE
LOCKED UP LIKE A CAVEMAN

OR,
FLIP, FLIP
SAVE
MAKE A HUNDRED GRAND
SELFMADE, CEO

RAP, A NIGGA EXCAPE ROUTE
FO, SHO!

My Mind

Fear is false evidence appearing real
a wise woman once informed me
dis-informed you
cause you refuse to study
think outside the box
"Jesus Can't Save You"
Jay-Z said
Subliminal Verse
Our Children rehearse
old school Cadillac hearse
like the one in the movie "love Jones"
decayed bones still rotting
I haven't forgotten
UN-paid wages
Mockery stages
new tune in the melody of Jazz
Those same who resemble "Us" can be against "Us"
like in the beginning of Alex Haley's "Roots"
so I'll shoot right to the point
the plot, and the scheme is so far beyond reach
as helpless citizen's we must teach
read threw the fine lines, start being on time
not for work you see
our government has great plans for you, and for me
sex, and skin color have been waived
we will all be slaves to a One World Government
you may not agree
But, your welcome to search
do your own research

I Watched the News

How can we protest?
Raise hell, open jails
If, the finger points, back at you?

My eyes bleed with fury
While court's don't pick jury's
for death, in the hands of "COP"

Better yet, the officers we call "PIGS"
Can you dig it?
Judicial system racial bigots!!

Before, I go there
Let's be fair
No sympathy can be given
If you're driven to Rob, Cheat, & Kill
Sit-ins, riots, and boycotts
Were represented by innocence
Not ignorance

These day's in time
Karma don't rhyme
We just suffer

Another, broth slain
On the streets

In jail Dustin'
The white man's feet
When will we see the sheets?
Invisible to the eye
But, I spy for us all

My Brotha's & Sista's make sure
We stand tall
Let's not be each other's downfall

The Ballet

Vote or Die
Slogan for 2004
Never said before
Then it changed to

Rock the Vote
I'm going with
Vote or Die!

Similar to Float or Drown

America is going down
Constitution being substituted
Like that irritating teacher
7th grade
Told my momma, I cursed aloud
She wasn't proud
Is it such a crime to vote again?
In the same ignorance, simply because he's black!
I don't think so
It's such a beautiful Look!

Never mind the lesser of two evils
For now

The world is yours

Just claim it
No shame in plotting
The fame
Beginnings of dictatorship
Communistic thinking
Come from these views
Sounds real shrewd
When everyone wants to rule
Steal votes
Cover up scandals
Execute culture
Imprison the innocent
I'm so speratic
Got to get combatic
But, I need a team
A discrete theme
Nothing is what it seems
So, this is just a DREAM.

Inquiring Minds . . .

Only the virtue of humanness
Can save humanity
Words of wise men
To control sin
Inherited hierchy
Deteriates society
Thought-provoking context
The material I read
Sends me to my calculations
Speculations . . . the journey to truth.

Generations

Most folk have no clue
Our generation Brand new
Branded by reality TV, Fashion & Fad
Today's up bringing so sad
Over emphasis on getting an education
But, no background information
Children of all creeds
Need knowledge of rooted seeds
What's education & wealth, without awareness of self?
Sight goes deeper than eyes
Need further emphasis
Descendants of 40 acres & a Mule, Trail of Tears,
Japanese containment camps, holocaust survivors,
So-called Mexican Immigrants
TEACH & PREACH
So when asked who?
Children know how to proudly say;

I am Tamara Allen
A descendant of the Cherokee Nation, by Robert & Lucy Allen,
my bloodline also traces back to the Blanton Plantation.
Which was, the slave master's last name
that branded my family,
The Blanton Plantation& burial ground for my family,
is located in East Texas, just 45minutes outside the state of Louisiana.

THE REST OF THIS POEM ENDS IN THE SEA,
HOWEVER I CAN STILL GO ON
MY ANCESTORS SAT ON THRONES,
FATHERED & MOTHERED THIS EARTH
FACES RESEMBLE THE SOIL &
THIS CONCEPT CREATES GREAT TURMOIL!

Sucker!

Words leak, but don't sink
Garbage disposal method
Ideal planted, then shredded
False hope, false prophets, false profit
All cash don't last
During the conversion
Ideal= Investment = product = consumer
Target those who don't got it
Who gone work hard, break necks
To afford
It's called the working class
Now class dismissed
Teaching w/no master's or bachelor's
Common sense = self defense
Still don't get it
Stop spending start saving!

The Dream Ticket

Wire tapped crickets
Not the insect, the cell phone
Some states a Metro
Census Bureau helps take count
And
By rule of thumbs
Countries form alliance
Barcode reliance
Access granted, opened borders
New world order
For the 666th time
Every major accomplishment
Mirrored by one great crime
1 Million Covered up lies
Only an estimate, new estimate ending

The order of Complicity
My words lack sympathy
For those who mourn, get re-born
Souls stay scorned
Super sized Churches
Mold minds like clay

I prefer my own acquired data
Don't matter anyway
We all got ass holes
Massive eyes closed!

No Solution

6.7 million used
1.3 received treatment
So emprision those who serve
What's in demand
Command, Control, Alt Delete
Quit's the application
If you want to end illegal drug distrubtion
Legalize
Since beginning of mankind
Folk been getting "High"
Rather it be earth grown mushrooms
Mademade meth
Extasay beaming you the the moon
So you thought . . . shyt
Sex a Drug
Work is a Drug
Food is a drug
Anything you use excessively
Due to your depression see
Even those happy want the high
Floating while standing still
Rather it be 2 seconds like Crack
Or Hours like a Double Stack Transformeer
Zebra print purple & pink power ranger
Consumers the dummies
Government posing like gumby

All friendly
They floating the shit in
W didn't land on Plymouth rock!
You heard it before, need I quote
Illegal drug distribution without a tax stamp
All "They" want is they Cut
D-Boys you boast and brag 10 a key
Add that six cent on a dollar
Pay the IRS
Greedy Uncle Sam
Green eggs & Ham
You Niggas still eating spam
Bullshit emails received
Just like dime dope sentences
Bleach don't cover blemishes
Damn My brotha
I know it's fast cash
That shit don't last
Can't beat the system that beats you
My Brutha, My King
I know nothing is what it seems
Everything aint got to be Dope Boy Dreams
Your worth so much more
Get it together OR
Your Business might = RICO

Dog Fights

Let me spit to ya soul
Smokers be ya mama
Grandma, brotha, sista, teacher
Sneaker representer,
Whatever
Endorsements get signed
Crimes get committed
Citizen's sigh
Discouraged
People just people
Even in the "lime light"
Dollar for dollar
Million after Million dollar contracts
Signed
White collar crimes
Get dime sentences
Sometimes
My rhymes
Fill ya soul
Currency originally gold
Truth scolds like hot water
3rd degree burns
Curling irons make for cute
Mascara lengthens eyelashes
Enemies clash
Fist from clashes clay

Mohammad Ali, in the end
Like the world was once viewed square,
Now seen round
Equal to frowns, turned to smiles
Crowds dead, now AWAKEN
Rock left, Rock right
Wave ya hands, fresh air!

Listen

THE NATURE OF CONTRIDICTION
FALSE PREDICTIONS
CREATED FICTION
USED AS PROPROGANDA
GENERATES MASS HYSTERIA
THE OZONE IS DEPLETED
THE GREENHOUSE IS HEATED
MOUNT WEATHER IS COMPLETED
UNITED NATIONS PRESENTS TREATY'S
DRUG LORDS GET GREEDY
THE POOR STILL NEEDY
WON'T ANY BODY BELIEVE ME?
EVERY PRESIDENCY
FURTHERED THE CAUSE
WE MUST TAKE A PAUSE
RE-CONSIDER THE DATA
GET READY FOR BATTLE
PROTECT OUR CATTLE
SO WE CAN EAT
REST OUR FEET
W/O SERIAL NUMBERS
PLACED FOR BRAND
BACK IN DEMAND

REBELS AND REVOLUTIONAIRIES
ADVERSARY'S OF THE GOVERNEMENT

Running But Standing still

LISTEN & ADHEAR
A QUEEN IS AT YOUR EAR

How did the Jews catch up?
Isn't that tough
"We" still playing catch up
Concentration camps
Disguised as showers & Bathrooms
Couldn't smell them gas fumes
6 million fractioned out
The Willie Lynch letter
Stated with accumulated time
How to keep the "black man" behind
Game time
No Kobe, No Tiger, No Shaq
Picture that
Baby's mommas lose weight, and then snap back
"We" still hooked on selling crack
"I think I'm Big Meech"
Mentality is so WACK
I can write all day, Talk for a year
But, will you adhere
We need to break this cycle
Not recycle the same set backs
African Americans in Positions of power
With sold souls

Does not represent change
Two Quarters, Four Dimes, and two Nickels
Equal one dollar
If we can't come together
Why bother?

To My Cyber Friends

You can loose everything
Nothing is more important than loosing life
Even after that
The measurement is
Loosing life—vs—loosing your life
In the midst of losing life
One may loose them self
At the same time, one may find self
However, loosing your own life
Ends everything, even if remembered like Dr. King
The Dream lives, and still fades
In due time
Self-Preservation is a must
A hard lesson learned
In this day in time, selfishness
Is the key . . .
IF one doesn't have for self, why help?
Those who give, still receive tax right offs
So Charity is for the "Good Look"
Katrina was created by Government crooks
Tsunami's swirl internationally
California will drown soon
No baby boom
Big Bang Theory, fake as cheap weave
You keep that on deck
What to do when bank accounts frozen?

Executive orders close grocery stores, gas, and electric
How will we survive during the battle of the fetus
Read revelations with understanding
There is a whole new era coming
How to get ready I don't even know
But, if you think simply going to Church, and Praying
Is the only answer
Then why is there no Cure for Cancer
I'm just saying
Great minds think alike, and I'd love to meet Spike
I love to meet YOU
We need a plan

METAMORPHOSIS
WITH IN

Terminated Empire

They can't even tell, I'm dying
Feeling like a clown, let down
Echo sound of failure
Everything true & fake at the same time
Try hard, die hard
Deck of cards, unrevealed
Envelopes sealed with saliva
Babies delivered through vaginas
Fat released in saunas
Reputations created through drama
Fate comes with Karma
Didn't listen to my mama
So, I struggle
Un-employed
College credits, but no degree
Million dollar empire flushed down the drain
Chamber of commerce
What's currency, without longevity?
A million spend like quarters
I seen it done
1.4 million So, they say
Our community un-concerned
Money run out, friends jump out!
Our family worked so hard
Only to be charged with fraud
While truly innocent

Sentenced to 92months in federal prison
Due to past felony's
Dated over 10 years back
Isn't that jacked?
Turn your back
Slip fall in a crack
deep down under
Need a plunger, from being sunk in
All though operated 15years independently
One wrong move while government funded
The government stunted
Like Baby n Manny Fresh
Deposited hundreds of thousands
As a set up
No training, no notated billing codes
Greedy foes exposed
Ironically
Murdered before testimony could be given
Money the root to all evil
Biblical term quoted "love of"
In this case I wish we would have stayed broke
Never got a dime
Then there never would have been a crime

A Piece Of Me

BY MYSELF
WHO DO I CALL ON?
NO SHOULDER TO LEAN ON
HOW CAN I MOVE ON?
TRAPPED IN TIME
WISH I COULD PRESS REWIND
WHEN FRIENDSHIP WAS REAL
TRUST WAS NO QUESTION
AND SOWARROWS WERE UN-REVEALED
MEMORIES LAST FOREVER
PICTURES SAVOR THE MOMENT
SCARS MARK THE HEART
THEN GRUDGES RULE THE SOUL
THE REAL STORY IS NEVER TOLD
LIES, AND DECIET LINGER IN THE AIR
NOTHING IS FAIR
HOW DO YOU KNOW IF YOU SHOULD BEWARE?
SOMEONE YOU THOUGHT YOU KNEW
SURELY HE WOULD NEVER hurt YOU
NOW WHAT DO YOU DO?

Terrie Said!

What can I say the real me eventually faded away
Now I'm condemned for every little step I take
Bobby B Voice
Mockery!
In
The depths of me
Lies . . .
One never ending poetic stanza
Various songs on repeat
I dance off beat
Un-controlling two left feet

All my ex's don't live in Texas
They live in blonde haired vaginas
Ha!
Like playing the dozens as kids
Don't get in ya feelings when I say this

It is not that I am Jealous
Insecure or racist
I certainly understand over coming the past
However, why my brother's forget so fast?
Emmitt Till only whistled aloud

Ended up in a closed casket

Catch my drift
Love is blind, because the money green
That is what the Brothers scream
Complaining black girls to mean
Well I say why, do you want a carbon copy of me?

Date the real thing!
Not the ones with the fake hip hop slang
I'm just saying
I did this one for fun!
Those that chose to laugh
Hell I'm laughing too,
What started as game, turned into your main

Change

A SILENT PATH
CALCULATED THE MATH
SEEKING FOR THE NEXT
THE SECURITY OF THE UNKNOWN
I AM BLESSED WITH
EVERY STEP CONSTANTLY BRAND NEW
ALWAYS A NEW LESSON LEARNED
DOESN'T ALWAYS SCORN
THE NEED FOR CONSISTANCY
I SEARCH FOR, WILL TO GAIN
STRAIN
FANATICIZE DAILY
SO, I HAVE DEDIDED
TO RIDE A NEW TURF, WITH A STRONGER GRIP
OKAY TO FALL, ONLY IF ONE STILL RISES
MY SOBREITY MAINTAINS ONLY BY SUCCESS
TOO MUCH DOWN TIMES
EMBRACED BINGE TIME
VACATIONING ON LONG ISLAND
IF IM MAD, THEN IT'S MAD DOG
CATCH ON
LIFE CERTAINLY GOES ON
THE ESSENCE OF NATURE
ALL GREATNESS COMBINED
VIBRATIONS CREATE THE NEGATIVE, OR POSITIVE
HEAVEN, OR HELL

STATE OF MIND
UNTIL MANKIND DESTROY'S
LIKE IN MOST PLOTTED ENDING'S
MOVIES
GOODNESS ALWAYS'S PREVAILS
HOPEFULLY IN REALITY TOO

Faces

The best memories never come back
So, I cut Nigga's slack
Fuck a grudge
Who can judge character?
Faces change so often
Not like one's in coffin's
But, those who be walk'n & talk'n
Smiling, and then frowning
I'll just holla every now & then
Furniture get rearranged & replaced
Compare it to life
Scenarios have sequels
Like arguments forgiven . . .

Murder 1

120 days
Released to
Sedgwick Co. Jail
Planning to Attend
The Trail
The Testimony
Words of His Story
Eyes Face to Face
Hopefully
Found Guilty
Pre-Meditated
First-Degree Murder
Man Slaughter
Watch what you call your self
Accredited nicknames
Becomes you
I Pray
You're sentenced
22 consecutive life sentences
Body just rots
Not to be removed
Punished eternally
All dreams gone
No second chance
Given
Never Forgiven

Not in my eyes
You snatched
My soul
Stole
My Breath
Can't Explain
The rest
His Family
I pray for God to Bless
Because of your unhappiness
No knowledge of higher self
Has all of us stressed
Caught in an awful Memory
"The Murder of Tellus J. Colvin"

Mind Daze

Situations that shape us
Life's thrusts
Unfair
Like those raped, but nobody believed them
I speak in 3rd
So that I may be heard
I truly wonder what is in store, our future
Thinking positive, is not equal to thinking realistic
I want to do more, because I know what most don't
What most will not research, read, or shout about
Fogged by life's clout
Keeps us all stagnant, content
I'm not talk'n drama folks
Facebook pokes
360 revolving days working, taking care of children, Family, bills
Adulthood so to speak
Keeps us playing to the tune
New York tribune
Details truth, get it?
Shit, I don't!
Why did the birds fall?
Midwest, did that equal test?

Definitely ignited quest
I'm sitting at my desk, evaluating & googling
Where is the real search mechanism?
Like faked orgasms, I get filtered results
Instead of one, united movement
Each educated or stimulated "Black" has its own movement
Saying follow me . . .
True intent sincere, but no organization
I along with many fear to join, or participate
To be an Indian, one must be able to trust the Chief
Chiefs are often thieves
These days in time
My thoughts bounce, words unpronounced have no meaning
On-line music streaming
Never do what they do
Roots,
And we can't trace them
The saga continues in this conspiracy archive
Sometimes I give up on the thought
Like now my ink ran out
I'll pick up on this later
Writers block

Observations of Me

Diary of a mad, angry
Bitter, lonely, depressed
Queen
Is this not the analysis?
They say I'm too independent
Never submissive
Overly defensive
But, did you ever think to wonder why?
Maybe it was all the times you cheated
The black eye
The bottle over my head
Pretending to be my friend
Poisoned by malt liquor
My skull should have been thicker
Cause I didn't see the rape coming
That was my fault
So, it's said
In college drinking Kentucky deluxe
Why so much?
TMI you might say
This is my damn pen
Now shall I began
Drowning in my past
Drenches my future
Guards are up double bolt lock
Mental pistol stays cocked

How do I shed out this skin?
Start a new begin
I think I'm cursed
My life previously rehearsed
I had no practice
Just fell in the katus, no tweezers
In order to understand this Queen
You must know my past
Don't judge me, hear me
Clearly vie been through a lot
Im not damaged
The exchange is easy
I know what I want
I know my self worth
If that makes me a mad, angry, bitter, depressed woman
Than, I guess I am

I Crowned My Damn Self!

I crowned my damn self
Bloodlines will not trace me to My Throne

I said I crowned my damn self
The seeds that grow into roots
Dissolved in someone else soil

Queendom is a state of mind

Only a certain kind dares to claim

This is not the Daughter of King George III
But, My name is Tamara

I aim at the crowds
Speaking aloud
Know they self, don't always focus
On tremendous wealth

So many of you just don't get it
Knowing self is similar to wining the lottery
Not knowing just plain robbery

Shit we can't convict the thief
I told you before
Crimes against humanity have no real re-precautions

We have a president to claim
Still no reparations

Obama's last name traces back to Kenya
Not no damn Virginia
So is the dream for filled, they continue ask
I say Hell NO
I had to Crown My Damn Self!

AND

I'll reign until I say
(Raises Voice)
Yeah I got an attitude!
I got some shit to say!

Still to this date 2012 "We" affected
From minority to majority
Still no voice, no true choice
Though thousands of petitions were signed
Troy Davis clemency was deigned

I Said!

I Crowned My Damn Self
I choose to inform
My Coat Of Arms
Internet Censorship
Soap Opera Act
Did you forget they Implanted
Crack
Our Communities
It's called Neutralization

Before that it was
Sterilization

They have tried it all
Deterioration of the resemblance of sand
Melonated skin tones
Original bones jotted down
Even though we can't trace it
Like Alex Haley's Roots

We Still Here

That's Why I Can Crown My Damn Self!!!!

www.ingramcontent.com/pod-product-compliance
Lightning Source LLC
Chambersburg PA
CBHW061310280526
45784CB00002B/949